April 2012

VA ADMINISTRATIVE INVESTIGATIONS

Improvements Needed in Collecting and Sharing Information

GAO
Accountability ★ Integrity ★ Reliability

GAO-12-483

April 2012

GAO
Accountability * Integrity * Reliability

Highlights

Highlights of GAO-12-483, a report to congressional requesters

VA ADMINISTRATIVE INVESTIGATIONS

Improvements Needed in Collecting and Sharing Information

Why GAO Did This Study

VA may use an AIB to determine the facts surrounding alleged employee misconduct or potential systemic deficiencies related to VA policies or procedures. AIBs do not determine corrective actions, such as individual disciplinary actions or procedural changes, but AIB investigation results, including evidence, may be used to inform such actions, making it critical for AIBs to be convened and conducted appropriately.

You expressed interest in the number of AIB investigations and their results. In this report, GAO examines (1) the process VA uses to convene and conduct AIB investigations, (2) the extent to which VA collects data on AIB investigations, and (3) how VA has used the results of its AIB investigations. GAO focused on AIB investigations conducted within VHA; reviewed VA documents, including policies and procedures, and VHA data on AIBs conducted during fiscal years 2009 through 2011; and interviewed VA officials from headquarters and four medical centers. To ensure data reliability, GAO reviewed VHA's methods to collect AIB data.

What GAO Recommends

GAO recommends that VA establish processes to (1) collect and analyze aggregate data from AIB investigations conducted within VHA, and (2) share information about improvements that are implemented in response to the results of AIB investigations. VA concurred with these recommendations.

View GAO-12-483. For more information, contact Debra A. Draper at (202) 512-7114 or draperd@gao.gov.

What GAO Found

The Department of Veterans Affairs (VA) has departmentwide policy and procedures for convening and conducting administrative investigation boards (AIB). The department's procedures contain requirements for convening and conducting AIB investigations, but according to VA officials, they also provide the flexibility to tailor an investigation to effectively meet diverse informational needs. For example, the VA official convening an AIB investigation is required to select AIB members who are impartial and objective, but has flexibility to vary the number of members appointed to each AIB based on the matter being investigated. VA is currently updating its AIB policy and procedures, but officials said the department plans to maintain flexibility in its AIB process.

VA does not collect and analyze aggregate data on AIB investigations, including data on the number of AIB investigations conducted, the types of matters investigated, and whether the matters were substantiated, or on any systemic deficiencies identified by AIBs. Having aggregate data could provide VA with valuable information to systematically gauge the extent to which matters investigated by AIBs may be occurring throughout VA's Veterans Health Administration (VHA) and to take corrective action, if needed, to reduce the likelihood of future occurrences. Without such data, VA is unable to adequately assess the causes or factors that may contribute to deficiencies occurring within its medical centers and health care networks. Information on AIB investigations is maintained by different offices across VA. For example, each medical center or network maintains information on each AIB investigation that it conducts. In response to GAO's request for AIB data, VHA administered a web-based survey that collected data from all its medical centers and networks on AIB investigations they reported conducting during fiscal years 2009 through 2011. Survey data showed that medical centers and networks conducted more than 1,100 investigations during this time period, and the types of matters investigated included allegations of inappropriate employee behavior involving patients and other employees; individual employee wrongdoing, such as theft and fraud; and systemic deficiencies. VHA officials told us that although it administered the web-based survey, the department has no plans to collect and analyze aggregate data on AIB investigations conducted within VHA.

VA has used the results of AIB investigations to inform corrective actions, but does not share information about improvements made that could have broader applicability. Specifically, VA has used the results of AIB investigations to inform systemic changes at the medical centers and networks where AIB investigations have been conducted. For example, VA has developed new policies and procedures for improving patient and employee safety and developed new training programs to expand employees' knowledge of VA policies and procedures. However, VA does not share information about these improvements that may have relevance for other areas within VHA. Such information could be used to improve not only the quality of patient care provided, but also the efficiency of VHA's overall operations. For example, one medical center included in GAO's review implemented a tracking system to ensure surgical instruments are delivered promptly to the operating room and a checklist to ensure the availability of needed equipment prior to starting surgery.

_____ **United States Government Accountability Office**

Contents

Abbreviations

AIB	administrative investigation board
GS	General Schedule
VA	Department of Veterans Affairs
VHA	Veterans Health Administration

United States Government Accountability Office
Washington, DC 20548

April 30, 2012

The Honorable Richard Burr
Ranking Member
Committee on Veterans' Affairs
United States Senate

The Honorable Brad Miller
House of Representatives

The Department of Veterans Affairs (VA) operates one of the largest
health care delivery systems in the nation. In fiscal year 2011, VA
provided health care services to about 6.2 million veterans through its
Veterans Health Administration (VHA), which consists of 153 medical
centers across 21 health care networks.[1] In fiscal year 2011, VHA
employed about 255,000 staff members at various levels including
managers, clinicians, and administrative staff.

For matters of alleged employee misconduct or potential systemic
deficiencies related to VA policies or procedures, VA may use an
administrative investigation board (AIB) as a tool to collect evidence and
determine the facts surrounding the matter being investigated. These
investigations may focus on alleged individual employee misconduct by
any VA staff member, regardless of level. AIB investigations may be
convened throughout VA, including its medical centers, networks, and
headquarters.

AIB investigations are important tools, as their results (evidence, findings,
conclusions, and recommendations) may be used to inform corrective
actions, whether individual disciplinary actions for employee misconduct,
or broader policy or procedural changes in cases of identified systemic
deficiencies.[2] Apart from AIB investigations, VA uses other tools to
identify potential areas for improvement. For example, related to issues of

---

[1]Each network, which VA refers to as a Veterans Integrated Service Network, is
responsible for management and oversight of its medical centers, which typically include
one or more hospitals as well as other types of health care facilities, such as outpatient
clinics and nursing homes.

[2]Although results from AIB investigations may be used by VA officials to inform corrective
actions, AIBs are not involved in determining or implementing any corrective actions.

GAO-12-483 VA Administrative Investigation Boards

patient safety, VA uses root cause analysis—a methodology for identifying the basic or contributing factors that underlie variations in the performance of systems and processes. However, AIB investigations serve a unique management role. Unlike information collected from these other tools, evidence collected by an AIB investigation may be used by management to inform employee disciplinary action.[3] Because of the potential implications for VA staff and systems, it is critical for AIBs to be convened and conducted appropriately. AIB investigations that do not adequately address critical issues, or that reach findings, conclusions, or recommendations not supported by the evidence, are an ineffective use of resources and may also adversely affect VA's operations and systems, including the quality of care provided in its medical centers; the morale of its employees; and its public image.

You expressed interest in VA's AIB investigations, including the number of investigations and their results. In this report, we focused on AIB investigations conducted in VHA, and examined: (1) the process VA uses to convene and conduct AIB investigations, (2) the extent to which VA collects data on AIB investigations, and (3) how VA has used the results of its AIB investigations.

To determine the process VA uses to convene and conduct AIB investigations, we reviewed VA documentation, including VA's policy and procedures for AIB investigations.[4] We also reviewed documentation and interviewed officials from three other federal agencies to gain an understanding of their administrations investigation processes, and how they compare to VA's process. Specifically, we selected the Federal Bureau of Prisons and the U.S. Navy Bureau of Medicine and Surgery because, like VA, these agencies provide health care services. We also selected the U.S. Coast Guard because VA officials told us that VA's AIB process was modeled after the Coast Guard's administrative investigation process. We interviewed officials from each of these federal agencies who were knowledgeable about their respective agency's administrative

---

[3]The information generated from root cause analysis and other tools is confidential and protected from disclosure within and outside of VA. See 38 U.S.C. § 5705; 38 C.F.R. §§ 17.500-17.511.

[4]VA Directive 0700, *Administrative Investigations* (Mar. 25, 2002) and VA Handbook 0700, *Administrative Investigations* (July 31, 2002) contain VA's policy and procedures, respectively, for AIB investigations.

GAO-12-483 VA Administrative Investigation Boards

investigation process. We did not evaluate these three federal agencies' processes for convening and conducting administrative investigations.

To determine the extent to which VA collects data on AIB investigations, and how VA has used the results of its AIB investigations, we interviewed VA officials about the type of data the department collects and maintains on these investigations. Although AIB investigations may be conducted throughout VA, we focused our review only on AIB investigations that were conducted within VHA. Additionally, we focused on AIB investigations conducted during fiscal years 2009 through 2011. In response to our request for AIB data, VHA administered a web-based survey that collected data from all its medical centers and networks on AIB investigations they reported conducting during fiscal years 2009 through 2011. We reviewed and analyzed the survey data on the number of AIB investigations. VA officials told us that data resulting from the survey included AIB investigations involving staff at the General Schedule (GS) -15 level and below,[5] but did not include AIB investigations involving senior leadership or matters related to research misconduct within VA medical centers or networks or within VHA headquarters.[6] Thus, for AIB investigations involving senior leadership and matters of research misconduct conducted during fiscal years 2009 through 2011, we collected and analyzed AIB data maintained by VHA's Office of Workforce Management and Consulting and Office of Research Oversight, respectively. We spoke with knowledgeable VHA officials about the data, including the methodology used to conduct the web-based survey, and their efforts to ensure the reliability of the data. Based on these discussions, and our review of related documentation we determined the data to be sufficiently reliable for our purposes. We did not evaluate the appropriateness of the number of AIB investigations conducted. Additionally, we reviewed VA-wide policy and procedures for taking disciplinary actions,[7] and specific VA policy and procedures for taking

---

[5]VA officials told us the data also included staff who are not paid under the GS system, such as physicians, dentists, and registered nurses. Throughout this report, we use the term "GS-15 level and below" to include these staff.

[6]VA defines senior leadership to include members of the senior executive service; associate and assistant directors, chiefs of staff, and nurse executives at its medical centers; heads of other VA offices such as networks; GS-15 or equivalent positions in VHA headquarters; and all other positions centralized to the Secretary.

[7]VA Directive 5021 and VA Handbook 5021, *Employee/Management Relations* (Apr. 15, 2002).

corrective actions against staff involved in research misconduct.[8] We also reviewed VA's processes related to AIB investigations, in light of federal internal control standards, as documented in GAO's *Standards for Internal Control in the Federal Government*.[9]

For all three objectives, we interviewed officials from VA's Office of Inspector General, Office of General Counsel, and Office of Human Resources Management, as well as officials from VHA's Office of the Principal Deputy Under Secretary for Health; Office of the Assistant Deputy Under Secretary for Health for Quality, Safety, and Value, including its National Center for Patient Safety; Office of Workforce Management and Consulting; Office of Research Oversight; and Office of the Medical Inspector. These interviews aided our understanding of VA's AIB process, as well as its root cause analysis and peer review processes,[10] and how VA officials have used the results of these tools to inform corrective actions. We also interviewed officials from four medical centers—VA Boston Healthcare System, Canandaigua (N.Y.) VA Medical Center, Miami VA Healthcare System, and VA Pittsburgh Healthcare System. These medical centers varied in terms of complexity,[11] size,[12] and the number of AIB investigations conducted during fiscal years 2009 through 2011. For each medical center, we interviewed human resources staff; the medical center director, who also served as the convening authority for the AIB investigations we reviewed during this time period; and staff who had served as AIB chairs, to obtain information about their experiences with the investigations. We also obtained and reviewed investigation reports and related documents to identify the types of matters investigated by AIBs and the corrective actions that were

---

[8]VHA Directive 1058, *Office of Research Oversight* (Feb. 9, 2009) and VHA Handbook 1058.2, *Research Misconduct* (May 4, 2005).

[9]GAO, *Standards for Internal Control in the Federal Government*, GAO/AIMD-00-21.3.1 (Washington, D.C.: November 1999).

[10]Peer review is an organized process carried out by an individual health care professional or committee of professionals to evaluate and make recommendations to improve the performance of other professionals.

[11]We used VA's assessment of complexity for fiscal year 2008, which the department determined using multiple variables, including patient volume, types of clinical programs offered, and number of education and research programs.

[12]Size refers to the number of patients served by the medical center in fiscal year 2010.

GAO-12-483 VA Administrative Investigation Boards

informed by AIB investigations conducted during fiscal years 2009 through 2011 from the four medical centers included in our review.

We conducted this performance audit from July 2011 to April 2012 in accordance with generally accepted government auditing standards. Those standards require that we plan and perform the audit to obtain sufficient, appropriate evidence to provide a reasonable basis for our findings and conclusions based on our audit objectives. We believe that the evidence obtained provides a reasonable basis for our findings and conclusions based on our audit objectives.

VA Has Departmentwide Policy for Convening and Conducting AIB Investigations

VA has departmentwide policy and procedures for convening and conducting AIB investigations.[13] According to VA Handbook 0700, the department's procedures are intended "to promote effectiveness and uniformity in the conduct and reporting of AIB investigations," among other things. The procedures outlined in the handbook are mandatory, except where otherwise indicated. According to VA officials, the policy and procedures achieve their intended purpose, while also providing VA convening authorities—medical center directors, or any authorities senior to them within networks or headquarters—sufficient flexibility and discretion to tailor an investigation to effectively meet diverse informational needs. For example, convening authorities are required to select AIB members who are impartial and objective, but they have flexibility to vary the number of members appointed to each AIB based on the matter being investigated.

Officials within VA's Office of General Counsel—the office responsible for the contents of VA's AIB policy and procedures—are currently reviewing and updating the AIB policy and procedures as required every 5 years by VA.[14] Although revisions to its AIB policy and procedures were not finalized by the time we issued this report, officials within VA's Office of

---

[13]VA medical centers also may have local policies to guide the AIB process at their respective medical centers. Two of the four medical centers included in our review had such local policies. Our review of these policies found that they did not include additional procedures for convening and conducting AIB investigations, but rather identified local resources, such as medical center officials responsible for coordinating training for AIB members and implementing corrective actions.

[14]VA Directive 6330, *Directives Management* (Feb. 26, 2009).

General Counsel said the department plans to maintain flexibility in its AIB process.

VA's AIB process begins with a convening authority determining the need for an AIB investigation. Once convened, the AIB collects evidence, which may include witness testimony, and documents its results in an investigation report. (See fig. 1 for an overview of VA's process for convening and conducting AIB investigations.)

Figure 1: VA's Administrative Investigation Process

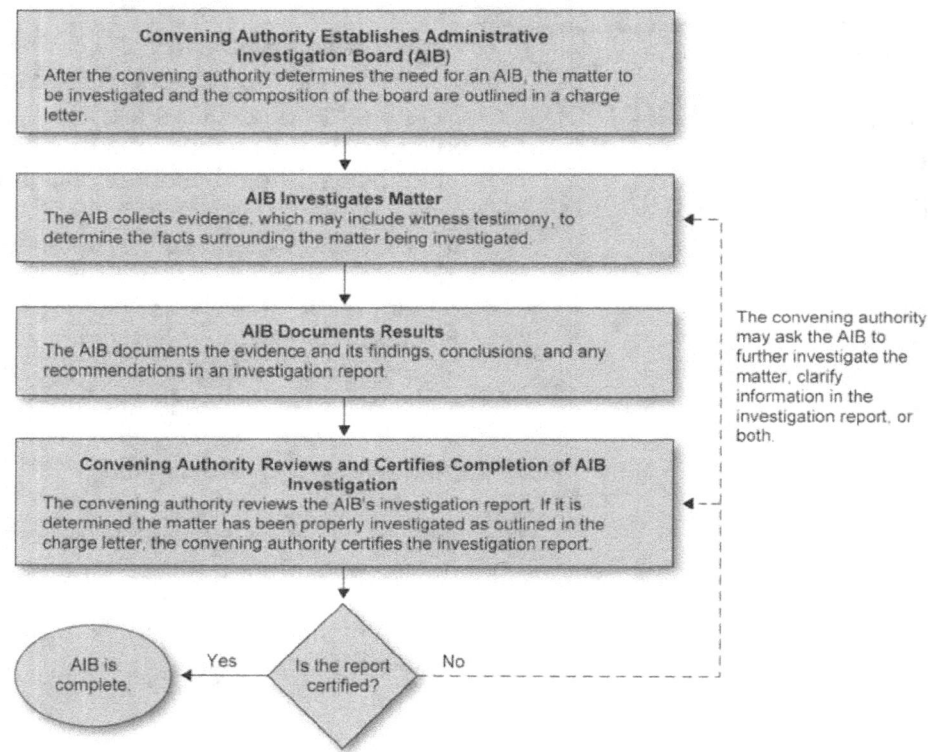

Source: GAO analysis of VA Handbook 0700 and AIB training materials, and interviews with VA officials.

GAO-12-483 VA Administrative Investigation Boards

Convening an AIB investigation involves determining its need, scope, and board composition. VA Handbook 0700 states that a convening authority may determine whether an AIB investigation is needed based on several factors, including the results of a preliminary investigation, any other ongoing investigation, or the type of matter being investigated.[15] A preliminary investigation is an informal process whereby readily available information is collected, for instance by obtaining witness statements. According to one convening authority, an AIB investigation would likely be convened after a preliminary investigation if, for example, conflicting witness accounts were provided during this initial investigation. A convening authority may also determine that another ongoing review into the matter, such as root cause analysis or peer review, meets VA's needs without convening an AIB.[16] Moreover, AIBs are not to investigate matters that may be criminal in nature without the convening authority first coordinating with federal and state law enforcement authorities, including VA's Office of Inspector General.[17]

A convening authority also determines the scope of the investigation and composition of the AIB. An investigation's scope—the matter to be investigated—may be focused on a specific incident involving alleged employee misconduct or a broader systemic matter. For example, among

---

[15]According to VA Handbook 0700, the decision to convene an AIB investigation should not be made by an official whose actions (or failure to act) may be a subject of the investigation, or who appears to have a personal stake or bias in the matter to be investigated.

[16]In some cases, even when a root cause analysis or peer review is being conducted, an AIB investigation may still be warranted. For example, an AIB may review a matter involving a medical procedure performed by a provider who may not have had the appropriate credentials or privileges. A root cause analysis also may be conducted on the same matter to review the medical center's processes for credentialing and privileging providers. Furthermore, an AIB may be convened, in addition to a root cause analysis or peer review, if evidence is needed to support potential employee disciplinary action, because the results of these reviews may not be used to inform such actions. According to VA, root cause analysis and peer review are generally not conducted concurrently with AIB investigations. If VA determines the need for an AIB investigation, because for example, there may have been an intentional act that led to an adverse event, any related root cause analysis or peer review is suspended or terminated. Additionally, information obtained from a root cause analysis or peer review is confidential and may not be used by an AIB. These reviews generate confidential records protected from disclosure within and outside of VA. See 38 U.S.C. § 5705; 38 C.F.R. §§ 17.500-17.511.

[17]VA management officials are required to report suspected criminal activity to the appropriate VA police or investigatory division, and are also required to report suspected felonies immediately to VA's Office of Inspector General. 38 C.F.R. §§ 1.203, 1.204.

the investigation reports we reviewed, one AIB investigated alleged physical and verbal abuse of a patient by a VA nursing assistant (an employee misconduct matter), while another investigated the facts and circumstances surrounding the death of a patient, including whether changes to policies and procedures were effectively communicated to staff and monitored (a systemic policy matter). In determining the composition of the AIB—the number and qualifications of members to be appointed—VA Handbook 0700 states that AIBs generally should be comprised of one to three members, and the members are to be selected primarily based on their expertise and investigative capability, as well as their objectivity and impartiality. Convening authorities we interviewed—medical center directors—said they typically appoint three members to ensure that AIBs include a subject matter expert and at least one member with investigative experience or training. Moreover, three of these convening authorities have appointed AIB members from outside their medical center when necessary to ensure the board's impartiality.

Finally, if the convening authority determines that an AIB is needed, it documents the AIB's scope and member composition in a charge letter, which officially authorizes the AIB investigation. During the course of the investigation, the convening authority may amend the charge letter, to change the scope of the investigation or composition of the AIB, among other things. For example, a convening authority included in our review initially charged an AIB to investigate an incident involving sexual harassment, but later expanded the investigation's scope to also include an incident involving reprisal against the individual who reported the harassment. According to one convening authority, it may be more cost effective to expand the scope of an investigation to address additional matters than to convene a second AIB. The charge letter also communicates any waivers to VA's procedural requirements for the AIB investigation. According to VA Handbook 0700, a convening authority may waive any of the requirements established by the handbook on a case-by-case basis, if, for example, requiring compliance with such requirements would not be cost effective.

The charge letter also may authorize the AIB to provide recommendations for corrective actions. According to VA Handbook 0700, an AIB only may provide recommendations if authorized to do so by the convening authority. However, an AIB is prohibited from recommending a specific level or type of corrective action, such as termination or suspension, and instead may only recommend "appropriate disciplinary action."[18] Moreover, although an AIB may provide recommendations, convening authorities are not required to implement them. Three of the four convening authorities we interviewed have authorized AIBs to provide recommendations, while one convening authority said that he generally has not because AIB members are not privy to all information pertaining to an employee who is the subject of the investigation, such as the individual's employment history.

After the investigation is convened, the AIB collects and analyzes evidence, such as witness testimony and documentation, related to the matter under investigation. An AIB may obtain witness testimony from VA employees, who are obligated to cooperate with the investigation,[19] as well as non-VA employees—including patients—who generally are not obligated to cooperate with the investigation. According to VA Handbook 0700, testimony may be obtained under oath and transcribed by tape recording, court reporter, or both.[20] Additionally, the AIB may obtain all available documents, records, and other information that are material to the scope of the investigation, including VA policies, employee personnel records, and e-mail correspondence.[21] The AIB analyzes the collected evidence and develops the findings and conclusions of the investigation, including whether any matter investigated was substantiated.[22]

The AIB documents results—evidence, findings, conclusions, and any recommendations—in an investigation report that is forwarded to the

[18]For AIB investigations related to research misconduct, AIBs are required to recommend corrective actions when the investigation finds that research misconduct has occurred.

[19]See 38 C.F.R § 0.735-12.

[20]Preliminary investigations, root cause analysis, and peer review do not obtain witness testimony under oath.

[21]Some information relevant to an investigation, such as patient medical records, may not be available to the AIB, or may be subject to specific restrictions on disclosure or use.

[22]According to VA Handbook 0700, AIB conclusions, such as whether a matter is substantiated, must be "based on at least a preponderance of the evidence."

convening authority.[23] The convening authority reviews the report to verify that the AIB sufficiently investigated the matter in accordance with the charge letter and VA's AIB policy.[24] The convening authority may ask the AIB to further investigate the matter, clarify the information in the investigation report, or both. VA considers an AIB investigation to be complete once the convening authority certifies the investigation report.

Similar to VA, three other federal agencies that we reviewed with administrative investigation processes—Federal Bureau of Prisons, U.S. Navy Bureau of Medicine and Surgery, and U.S. Coast Guard—have policies and procedures in place to guide their administrative investigations. Further, the results of these agencies' administrative investigations may be used to inform individual or systemic corrective actions. However, the extent to which the administrative investigations are expected to provide recommendations for such corrective actions varies by agency. (See app. I for characteristics of VA's and these three other federal agencies' administrative investigation processes.)

---

[23]VA Handbook 0700 states that each AIB member is to sign the investigation report, which confirms that each finding, conclusion, and recommendation (if included) is agreed upon by a majority of the members. AIB members who disagree with any of the findings, conclusions, and recommendations should attach a separate opinion identifying the area of disagreement.

[24]A convening authority also may document any waiver to the requirements of VA's AIB policy and procedures in the certification of the investigation report if this has not already been included in the charge letter.

VA Does Not Collect and Analyze Aggregate Data on AIB Investigations or the Deficiencies They Identify

VA does not collect and analyze aggregate data on AIB investigations, including data on the number of AIB investigations conducted, the types of matters investigated, and whether the matters were substantiated, or on any systemic deficiencies identified by AIBs. Without these data, VA is unable to adequately assess the causes or factors that may contribute to deficiencies occurring within all of its medical centers and networks.[25]

In contrast, through VA's Patient Safety Program,[26] VA collects and analyzes aggregate data on patient safety matters. When an adverse event involving patient safety occurs at a medical center, information about the event is entered into a tracking system that allows VA to electronically monitor patient safety information throughout its health care system. Additionally, some of these events are assessed through root cause analysis to determine the underlying causes of the adverse event and to develop and implement corrective action plans to reduce the likelihood of recurrence at the medical center, as well as the potential occurrence at other medical centers.

Information on AIB investigations is maintained by different offices across VA. For example, each medical center or network maintains the investigation report for each AIB investigation that it conducts related to VHA staff at the GS-15 level and below. In the absence of having aggregate data on AIB investigations, VHA administered a web-based survey to medical centers and networks, in response to our request for AIB data. These survey data on AIB investigations involving staff at the GS-15 level and below, in conjunction with VA data on AIB investigations involving senior leadership, showed that VHA conducted 1,143 AIB investigations during fiscal years 2009 through 2011.[27] (See table 1.)

---

[25]According to federal internal control standards, relevant, reliable, and timely information is needed throughout an agency to achieve its objectives and to control its operations. See GAO, *Standards for Internal Control in the Federal Government*, GAO/AIMD-00-21.3.1 (Washington, D.C.: November 1999).

[26]VA's Patient Safety Program is designed to identify and fix system flaws that could harm patients.

[27]These investigations do not include matters involving allegations of research misconduct. Data on AIB investigations involving these types of matters are maintained separately by VHA's Office of Research Oversight, which reported that medical centers conducted a total of eight investigations involving allegations of research misconduct during fiscal years 2009 through 2011. According to VHA officials, this office does not maintain data on the level of staff involved in these investigations.

Most of these investigations involved staff at the GS-15 level and below. VHA officials told us that although it administered the web-based survey in response to our request for data, the department has no plans to collect and analyze aggregate data on AIB investigations conducted within VHA.

Table 1: Number of Administrative Investigation Boards Conducted in VHA during Fiscal Years 2009 through 2011

VA staff level	Number of investigations conducted by VHA headquarters	Number of investigations conducted by medical centers and networks	Total
GS-15 and below[a]	1	1,113	1,114
Senior leadership[b]	6	23	29
Total	7	1,136	1,143

Source: GAO analysis of VA data.

Note: The data do not include administrative investigations involving allegations of research misconduct because VHA's Office of Research Oversight does not collect information on the level of staff involved in these investigations. VHA's Office of Research Oversight reported that medical centers conducted a total of eight investigations involving allegations of research misconduct during fiscal years 2009 through 2011.

[a]VA officials told us the data also included staff who are not paid under the GS system, such as physicians, dentists, and registered nurses. Additionally, these data do not include investigations involving GS-15 staff in VHA headquarters, and any investigations involving this level of staff would be included within data for senior leadership.

[b]VA defines senior leadership to include members of the senior executive service; associate and assistant directors, chiefs of staff, and nurse executives at its medical centers; heads of other VA offices such as networks; GS-15 or equivalent positions in VHA headquarters; and all other positions centralized to the Secretary.

According to the VHA survey data, the types of matters investigated by AIBs during fiscal years 2009 through 2011 included inappropriate employee behavior involving patients and other employees; individual employee wrongdoing, such as theft and fraud; and systemic deficiencies.[28] Our analysis of AIB investigation reports from the four medical centers in our review showed that allegations of inappropriate employee behavior involving patients and other employees were the most common types of matters investigated by AIBs during fiscal years 2009 through 2011. (See table 2 for more information on the types of matters

---

[28]VHA's survey data did not include examples of the types of systemic deficiencies investigated by AIBs.

investigated by AIBs at the four VA medical centers included in our review during fiscal years 2009 through 2011.)

Table 2: Types of Matters Investigated by Administrative Investigation Boards at Four Selected VA Medical Centers during Fiscal Years 2009 through 2011

Types of matters investigated	Description	Number
Inappropriate employee behavior involving patients	Sexual abuse, physical abuse, verbal abuse, unspecified patient abuse, patient death, patient safety, sexual harassment, or other matters such as employees accepting gifts from patients.	24
Inappropriate employee behavior involving other employees	Supervisory misconduct or sexual harassment.	13
Unclear VA policies or procedures, or violations of policies or procedures	Systemic deficiencies involving unclear policies or procedures that may have resulted in an injury to an employee or patient; as well as employees' lack of adherence to VA policies and procedures.	12
Individual employee wrongdoing	Theft or fraud by an employee.	7
Other	Matters that do not fit in any other category, such as missing medical equipment.	11
Total		**67**

Source: GAO analysis of VA documents.

Notes: During fiscal years 2009 through 2011, the four VA medical centers included in our review conducted a total of 49 administrative investigations. The total number of matters investigated is more than the total number of investigations conducted during this time period because some boards investigated more than one type of matter.

The data do not include administrative investigations involving matters of alleged research misconduct. VHA's Office of Research Oversight reported that two of the eight administrative investigations involving allegations of research misconduct occurred at a medical center included in our review.

VA Has Used the Results of AIB Investigations to Inform Corrective Actions, but Does Not Share Information about Improvements More Broadly

VA has used the results of AIB investigations to inform corrective actions taken at individual medical centers and networks to address both individual employee misconduct and system deficiencies. However, the department does not share information about improvements made in response to AIB investigations conducted at certain medical centers and networks that could have broader applicability.

VA Has Used the Results of AIB Investigations to Inform Corrective Actions against Individual Employees

To address matters of employee misconduct, VA has used the results of AIB investigations—evidence, findings, conclusions, and recommendations—along with other factors to inform corrective actions taken against individual employees.[29] These corrective actions range from disciplinary actions, such as termination or demotion, to nondisciplinary actions, such as counseling, reassignment, or training to expand an employee's knowledge about VA policies and procedures or clinical standards, according to information provided by VA officials we interviewed.[30] Although AIBs may make recommendations for corrective actions, they are not involved in determining actual corrective actions taken against an individual.

A medical center director or appropriate higher level official may use results from the investigation to help determine whether any corrective actions are warranted, and if so, the type and severity of each action. Other VA staff, such as human resources and general counsel staff, may also provide guidance to management in determining appropriate corrective actions. Specifically, in determining the type and severity of corrective actions to be taken, VA officials review the results of the AIB investigations, along with other factors related to the alleged misconduct being investigated, including the nature and seriousness of the offense, whether the conduct was intentional or inadvertent, and the type of penalty used for similar matters. VA officials also consider other information regarding an employee's history and conduct, including violations of VA policies. For example, medical center officials told us that an employee's history of time and attendance violations may be used in addition to the misconduct investigated by the AIB to inform disciplinary action against an employee.

VA does not collect and analyze aggregate information on the specific employee corrective actions that were informed by AIB investigations. Instead, this information is maintained by different offices throughout VA,

---

[29]For the subset of corrective actions that are disciplinary, according to VA's Office of General Counsel, VA may use the evidence obtained through an AIB, but may not use the findings, conclusions, or recommendations as support for, or to defend appeals of, disciplinary actions. For all other corrective actions, VA may use all the results (evidence, findings, conclusions, and recommendations) obtained through an AIB.

[30]The corrective action categories are based on our analysis of information provided by VA officials, including VA Directive 5021, VA Handbook 5021, and information VHA collected through its web-based survey.

including human resources offices at VA medical centers.[31] Information provided by VA officials from the medical centers included in our review showed that the results of the 49 AIB investigations conducted during fiscal years 2009 through 2011 have been used, along with other information, to inform 67 employee corrective actions.[32] (See table 3.) Suspension and training were among the most common corrective actions that were informed by AIB investigations taken at these medical centers.

[31]Although information on disciplinary corrective actions taken regarding matters of research misconduct is maintained by the medical center where the employee is located, information on nondisciplinary actions taken on these matters is maintained at VHA's Office of Research Oversight. For the eight research misconduct investigations conducted during fiscal years 2009 through 2011, VA officials reported that no corrective actions were taken for three of these investigations. For two investigations, the employees involved in the alleged misconduct resigned, and for three investigations, several corrective actions were taken, including an employee 30-day suspension, retraction of research articles, a 3-year prohibition against conducting research, and periodic and routine evaluations of the collection and reporting of research data for certain studies.

[32]VA's information did not include the total number of VHA staff who had action taken against them, but rather the number of corrective actions taken. Individuals could have had more than one corrective action taken against them and a single AIB investigation could have informed corrective actions against multiple individuals.

Table 3: Number of Employee Corrective Actions That Were Informed by Administrative Investigation Boards Conducted at Four Selected VA Medical Centers during Fiscal Years 2009 through 2011

Corrective action	Description	Total
Disciplinary action		
Termination	Involuntary separation of an employee from VA employment.	5
Suspension	Involuntary placement of an employee, for disciplinary reasons, in a non-duty, non-pay status for a period of time.	13
Demotion	Involuntary reduction in grade, reduction in basic pay based on conduct or performance.	2
Reprimand	Official letter of censure to an employee for major acts of misconduct or deficiency in competence. This letter usually remains in the employee's personnel folder for 3 years.	0
Admonishment	Official letter of censure to an employee for minor acts of misconduct or deficiency in competence. This letter usually remains in the employee's personnel folder for 2 years.	1
Nondisciplinary action		
Counseling	Verbal or written information intended to address an employee's conduct or performance.	4
Reassignment	An involuntary change in assignment to a different position, location, or both.	10
Training	Training to expand an employee's knowledge of current or new policies and procedures or clinical standards.	21
Other	Actions that do not fit in the corrective actions listed above or that were not specified.	11
Total		**67**

Source: GAO analysis of VA documents.

Notes: The corrective action categories are based on our analysis of information provided by VA officials, including VA Directive 5021, VA Handbook 5021, and information VHA collected through its web-based survey. These corrective actions do not result directly from administrative investigation boards (AIB), but rather the results of AIB investigations, along with other information available to VA officials, are used to inform the type of corrective action taken. For the subset of corrective actions that are disciplinary, according to VA's Office of General Counsel, VA may use the evidence obtained through an AIB, but may not use the findings, conclusions, or recommendations as support for, or to defend appeals of, disciplinary actions. For all other corrective actions, VA may use all the results obtained through an AIB.

VA's information did not include the total number of VHA staff who had action taken against them, but rather the number of corrective actions taken. Individuals could have had more than one corrective action taken against them and a single AIB investigation could have informed corrective actions against multiple individuals.

According to VA officials, no employee corrective actions were taken for the two research misconduct investigations conducted by a medical center included in our review as the alleged research misconduct matters in these investigations were not substantiated.

VA Has Used Results of AIB Investigations to Inform Systemic Changes at Individual Medical Centers and Networks, but Does Not Share Information More Broadly

In addition to informing employee corrective actions, VA has used the results of AIB investigations to inform corrective actions related to systemic changes at medical centers and networks where AIB investigations have been conducted.[33] Specifically, VA has developed new policies and procedures for improving patient and employee safety, developed new training programs to ensure employees' knowledge of VA policies and procedures, and implemented new or increased oversight of medical processes. For example, one medical center in our review used an AIB's findings of missing surgical instruments to support implementation of a tracking system to ensure the necessary surgical instruments are delivered promptly to the operating room and the development and implementation of a checklist to ensure the availability of needed equipment prior to starting surgery. This medical center also developed new procedures and annual training for clinical staff on the use of E-oxygen tanks—large aluminum cylinders that store compressed oxygen for medical use—in response to an AIB's findings that certain medical center staff did not know how to provide oxygen to a patient.

However, VA does not share information about systemic changes that are made in response to the results of AIB investigations that may have relevance for other areas within VHA.[34] Although two of the four medical center directors we interviewed told us they occasionally have shared information about changes made in response to AIB investigations they convened with other medical centers within their networks or with VA headquarters, this sharing has not routinely or systematically been done.

In contrast, as part of VA's overall efforts to report and address significant matters that affect its operations, VA tracks and shares information from root cause analyses it has performed. For example, information gathered from root cause analyses has been used by VA's Patient Safety Program to disseminate notices—alerts and advisories—to medical centers when actual or potential threats to the health and safety of patients have been

---

[33]VA may take employee corrective actions, as well as corrective actions related to identified systemic deficiencies in response to results from the same AIB investigation.

[34]According to federal internal control standards, information sharing between organizational components is an essential part of ensuring an effective and efficient use of resources. See GAO, *Standards for Internal Control in the Federal Government*, GAO/AIMD-00-21.3.1 (Washington, D.C.: November 1999).

identified.[35] These notices contain information about the patient safety matter, including actions taken, and any new procedures required. For example, in fiscal year 2011, following a root cause analysis, VA issued an alert regarding the safety of patients in mental health units who were using devices such as walkers to obstruct entry to their rooms. As part of this alert, VA directed its medical centers to take certain actions to ensure the safety of patients admitted to their mental health units. According to VA officials, VA's alerts and advisories are designed to focus attention on specific high-risk situations, such as medical equipment that may unintentionally harm patients or an unanticipated malfunction of a key piece of clinical software. For situations that are not considered high risk, VA's Patient Safety Program uses other information-sharing processes, including presentations, conference calls, or publications, to disseminate information about lessons learned. However, VHA officials told us that the department does not have similar processes for sharing information learned from AIB investigations. VHA officials said they rely on medical center and network leadership to identify and share such information.

Conclusions

AIBs are an important investigation tool for VA that can lead to operational improvements, including improved quality of care provided to veterans. However, VA neither collects nor analyzes aggregate data on AIB investigations nor does it routinely share information about systemic deficiencies identified or corrective actions taken to improve VHA operations and services. During fiscal years 2009 through 2011, VHA conducted more than 1,100 AIB investigations, yet the lack of such information from AIB investigations may result in missed opportunities for VA to gauge the extent to which deficiencies occur throughout its medical centers and networks to prevent escalation of problems, and to take timely corrective action, when needed. Such missed opportunities come with a cost when information from these investigations is not used to improve the quality and efficiency of VHA operations, including the delivery of care to veterans.

---

[35]Alerts disseminate urgent notices that require specific, mandatory, and timely action. Advisories are issued when a potential threat due to equipment design, procedural issues, or training has been identified. These advisories provide general recommendations for medical center directors, who must either implement these recommendations or implement procedures that provide equivalent or a higher level of safety than the recommendations provided in the advisory notices.

Recommendations for Executive Action

To systematically gauge the extent to which deficiencies identified by individual AIBs may be occurring throughout VHA; and to maximize opportunities for sharing information across VHA to improve its overall operations, we recommend that the Secretary of Veterans Affairs direct the Under Secretary for Health to take the following two actions for AIB investigations conducted within VHA:

- establish a process to collect and analyze aggregate data from AIB investigations, including the number of investigations conducted, the types of matters investigated, whether the matters were substantiated, and systemic deficiencies identified; and

- establish a process for sharing information about systemic changes, including policies and procedures implemented in response to the results of AIB investigations, which may have broader applicability throughout VHA.

Agency Comments and Our Evaluation

We provided a draft of this report to VA for comment. In its response, which is reprinted in appendix II, VA concurred with our recommendations. In its comments, VA identified several activities that VHA uses to identify, address, and share information about systemic issues in facilities and VHA program offices—including root cause analysis and peer review, which we discuss in our report. VA stated that it is within the context of these existing activities, which address quality and safety issues, that it would explore any new processes for collecting and analyzing aggregate data from AIB investigations. We believe that it is important for VA to establish such processes, even if they are processes within existing activities, to systematically gauge the extent to which deficiencies identified by individual AIBs may be occurring throughout VHA and to maximize opportunities for sharing information across VHA to improve its overall operations.

Additionally, VA stated that its comments focus only on implications and issues involving VHA, rather than VA, and suggested a revision to our recommendations to reflect this. As stated in the scope and methodology of this report, we focused on AIB investigations conducted in VHA, and thus our recommendations were only focused on these investigations. We revised the wording of our recommendation to clarify that we were focusing only on AIB investigations conducted within VHA. (VA also provided technical comments, which we have incorporated as appropriate.)

As agreed with your offices, unless you publicly announce the contents of this report earlier, we plan no further distribution until 30 days from the report date. At that time, we will send a copy of this report to the appropriate congressional committees and the Secretary of Veterans Affairs. The report also will be available at no charge on GAO's website at http://www.gao.gov.

If you or your staff have any questions about this report, please contact me at (202) 512-7114 or draperd@gao.gov. Contact points for our Offices of Congressional Relations and Public Affairs may be found on the last page of this report. GAO staff who made key contributions to this report are listed in appendix III.

Debra A. Draper
Director, Health Care

Appendix I: Characteristics of Selected Federal Agencies' Administrative Investigation Processes

Characteristic of administrative investigation processes	Department of Veterans Affairs	Federal Bureau of Prisons	U.S. Navy Bureau of Medicine and Surgery	U.S. Coast Guard
Requirement for conducting administrative investigations	Administrative investigations are to be conducted in accordance with departmentwide policy and procedures, which allow flexibility to tailor an investigation to meet diverse informational needs.	Administrative investigations must be conducted in accordance with agencywide policy.	Administrative investigations must be conducted in accordance with Navy-wide policy.	Administrative investigations must be conducted in accordance with agencywide policy.
Process for convening administrative investigations	A convening authority—medical center directors or any authority senior to them within networks or headquarters—determines the need and scope of the investigation based on several factors that may include the results of a preliminary investigation.	Matters are sorted into three categories based on their severity and potential consequences. Officials use these categories to determine whether an administrative investigation will be convened by the local institution or by another office in the agency or Department of Justice, such as the Office of the Inspector General.	A convening authority—usually a commanding officer—initiates a preliminary investigation into an incident. Based in part on the findings of the preliminary investigation, and in consultation with a Navy legal advisor, the convening authority may authorize an administrative investigation and if so, determines the scope of the investigation.	A convening authority—usually a senior officer—generally determines the need and scope of administrative investigations. For certain matters, such as fires or ship collisions, administrative investigations are required.
Process for selecting individuals to conduct administrative investigations	The convening authority selects individuals primarily based on their expertise and investigative capability, as well as their objectivity and impartiality. Generally, between one and three individuals should be selected to conduct the investigation.	Typically one individual designated from the institution's Special Investigator Supervisor Office—which primarily investigates crimes and corruption related to inmates and staff—conducts administrative investigations.	The convening authority selects one or more best-qualified individuals to conduct an administrative investigation based on age, education, training, experience, length of service, and temperament.	The convening authority selects the appropriate investigating officer. Typically, one junior officer conducts the investigation, but more officers may be appointed for complex incidents.

Characteristic of administrative investigation processes	Department of Veterans Affairs	Federal Bureau of Prisons	U.S. Navy Bureau of Medicine and Surgery	U.S. Coast Guard
Process for documenting results from administrative investigations	Investigation results are documented in an investigation report that includes the evidence, findings, conclusions, and any recommendations. The convening authority reviews the investigation report and certifies the investigation as complete.	Investigation results are documented in an investigation report that includes findings and conclusions. The Bureau of Prison's Office of Internal Affairs reviews the investigation report and closes the administrative investigation.	Investigation results are documented in an investigation report that includes findings of fact, opinions, conclusions, and any recommendations. The convening authority reviews and certifies the investigation report.	Investigation results are documented in an investigation report that includes findings, opinions, and recommendations. The convening authority reviews the investigation report. Any officer senior to the convening authority may also review the investigation report.
Expectation for administrative investigations reports to include recommendations	Administrative investigation reports may provide recommendations for corrective action if authorized to do so by the convening authority.	Administrative investigation reports do not provide recommendations for disciplinary action, but may provide recommendations for other corrective actions, such as employee training.	Administrative investigation reports may provide recommendations for corrective action only when requested to do so by the convening authority.	Administrative investigation reports are expected to provide recommendations for corrective action.

Source: GAO analysis of administrative investigation policies and procedures, and interviews with officials from the Department of Veterans Affairs, Federal Bureau of Prisons, U.S. Navy Bureau of Medicine and Surgery, and U.S. Coast Guard.

Appendix II: Comments from the Department of Veterans Affairs

DEPARTMENT OF VETERANS AFFAIRS
Washington DC 20420

April 12, 2012

Ms. Debra A. Draper
Director, Health Care
U.S. Government Accountability Office
441 G Street, NW
Washington, DC 20548

Dear Ms. Draper:

The Department of Veterans Affairs (VA) has reviewed the Government Accountability Office's (GAO) draft report, *"VA ADMINISTRATIVE INVESTIGATIONS: Improvements Needed in Collecting and Sharing Information"* (GAO-12-483). As discussed in the enclosed comments and as previously discussed with GAO staff, VA agrees that GAO's recommendations regarding the collection and analysis of aggregated data about the results of Administrative Investigation Boards (AIB) across the Veterans Health Administration (VHA) and sharing information about systemic changes identified in the AIB reviews merit further consideration

GAO's review focused on how the AIB process is implemented in VHA. Because the Under Secretary for Health does not have authority to establish programs throughout VA, this response focuses only on implications and issues involving VHA, rather than VA. The enclosure includes a suggested revision of the recommendations to reflect this limitation.

VA agrees that the AIB process is one important tool in VA's large toolkit of instruments used to collect and analyze data and subsequently address systemic issues. These tools and processes allow VHA to assess causes and factors that may contribute to deficiencies occurring in VA medical centers or in Veterans Integrated Service Networks as well as to identify system-wide policy implications and concerns. The enclosure outlines several additional tools that VHA uses to collect information about systemic and individual issues that occur at the facility level, including analyses that are done using information collected with these tools and how results are communicated throughout VHA. It is within the context of VHA's broad system of existing reviews and reports that we would explore any new processes for collecting and analyzing aggregate data from AIB investigations and whether such data may provide unique information that is crucial and not reported elsewhere.

The enclosure specifically addresses GAO's two recommendations and notes how the Department proposes to proceed. General and Technical comments are also provided. VA appreciates the opportunity to comment on your draft report.

Sincerely,

John R. Gingrich
Chief of Staff

Enclosure

Enclosure

Department of Veterans Affairs (VA) Comments to
Government Accountability Office (GAO) Draft Report
*"VA ADMINISTRATIVE INVESTIGATIONS: Improvements Needed in
Collecting and Sharing Information"*
(GAO-12-483)

<u>GAO Recommendation:</u> **To systematically gauge the extent to which deficiencies
identified by individual AIBs may be occurring throughout VA; and to maximize
opportunities for sharing information across the department to improve its
overall operations, we recommend that the Secretary of Veterans Affairs direct
the Under Secretary for Health to take the following two actions:**

<u>VA Comment:</u> Because the GAO review focused on how the Administrative
Investigation Board (AIB) process is implemented in the Veterans Health Administration
(VHA), and because the Under Secretary for Health (USH) does not have authority to
establish programs throughout VA, VA recommends that GAO revise language for the
recommendation as proposed below:

<u>Recommended revision:</u>

While the Administrative Investigation Board (AIB) process is used throughout the
Department of Veterans Affairs (VA), this Government Accountability Office (GAO)
review focused on the use of the AIB process only in the Veterans Health Administration
(VHA). To systematically gauge the extent to which deficiencies identified by individual
AIBs may be occurring throughout VHA, and to maximize opportunities for sharing
information across VHA, we recommend that the Secretary of Veterans Affairs direct the
Under Secretary for Health to take the following two actions:

> Explore the establishment of a process to collect and aggregate data from AIB
> investigations in VHA, including the number of investigations conducted, the
> types of matters investigated, whether the matters were substantiated, and
> systematic deficiencies identified; and

> Explore the establishment of a process for sharing information within VHA about
> systemic changes, including policies and procedures implemented in response to
> the results of AIB investigations in VHA, which may have broader applicability
> throughout VHA.

1

Enclosure

Department of Veterans Affairs (VA) Comments to
Government Accountability Office (GAO) Draft Report
*"VA ADMINISTRATIVE INVESTIGATIONS: Improvements Needed in
Collecting and Sharing Information"*
(GAO-12-483)

**Recommendation 1: Establish a process to collect and analyze aggregate data
from AIB investigations, including the number of investigations conducted, the
types of matters investigated, whether the matters were substantiated, and
systemic deficiencies identified.**

VA Comments: Concur with comments. VHA agrees that there is value in exploring the
usefulness of establishing processes to collect and analyze aggregated data from AIB
investigations. It is also important to note that other VHA processes, which would
normally occur prior to the conclusion of an AIB, require reporting and sharing
information when patient safety or other clinical issues are involved.

VHA will explore establishing processes to collect and analyze aggregate data from AIB
investigations to determine if the results of AIB reviews provide additional perspectives
that are not captured elsewhere. VHA officials have already begun discussions to
evaluate the merit of collecting and analyzing aggregated data, and we intend to use the
results of this GAO review to inform these discussions.
VHA expects to report its conclusions to the Secretary of Veterans Affairs no later than
September 30, 2012.

**Recommendation 2: Establish a process for sharing information about systemic
changes, including policies and procedures implemented in response to the
results of AIB investigations, which may have broader applicability throughout
the department, including its medical centers and networks.**

VA Comments: Concur with comments. VHA strongly agrees with the concept of
sharing information if any process identifies an issue that is of concern across VHA. It
is also important to note that other VHA processes, which would normally occur prior to
the conclusion of an AIB, require reporting and sharing information when patient safety
or other clinical issues are involved.

VHA will explore establishing processes to collect and analyze aggregate data from AIB
investigations to determine if the results of AIB reviews provide additional perspectives
that are not captured elsewhere. VHA officials have already begun discussions to
evaluate the merit of collecting and analyzing aggregated data, and we intend to use the
results of this GAO review to inform these discussions.

VHA expects to report its conclusions to the Secretary of Veterans Affairs no later than
September 30, 2012.

2

Department of Veterans Affairs (VA) Comments to
Government Accountability Office (GAO) Draft Report
**"VA ADMINISTRATIVE INVESTIGATIONS: Improvements Needed in
Collecting and Sharing Information"**
(GAO-12-483)

General comments:

**VHA Activities that Identify, Address, and Share Information about Systemic
Issues Identified in Facilities and VHA Program Offices**

The Veterans Health Administration (VHA) identifies, addresses, and shares information
about systemic issues identified in facilities and VHA program offices through numerous
processes, policies, tools, reports, and other methods, both proactive and reactive.
Examples include:

General. Information relative to quality, safety, and patient satisfaction are collected
and the data are shared internally and with the public:

- VA performance is posted on the Department of Health and Human Services
  (HHS), Centers for Medicare and Medicaid Services (CMS) Hospital Compare
  Web site (www.hospitalcompare.hhs.gov) and VA-specific sites
  (www.hospitalcompare.va.gov and www.qualityofcare.va.gov).

- The VHA quality and safety reports are published at
  http://www.va.gov/health/HospitalReportCard.asp.

Medical Inspector Reports. When a complaint or situation is brought to the Office of the
Medical Inspector (OMI), the results of the OMI review involving systemic issues are
shared with VHA Central Office (VHACO) policy and operations leadership and staff
(e.g., Offices of the Deputy Under Secretary for Health for Operations and Management
(DUSHOM) and DUSH for Policy and Services).

Issue Briefs. Facilities generate a description of a problem that is the result of an
unexpected incident in the facility through an Issue Brief (IB). An IB is generated at a
facility and reported through the relevant Veterans Integrated Service Network (VISN) to
the DUSHOM. An IB is shared as needed in VHACO and throughout VHA. An IB is
used to address individual and system issues.

Root Cause Analysis. Root Cause Analyses (RCA), which are designed and used as
tools for identifying prevention strategies, are conducted at VA medical centers (VAMC)
nationwide and entered into the VA's National Center for Patient Safety (NCPS) Patient
Safety Information System so that data are available to analyze patient safety
information across VHA. Lessons learned through RCAs are used to benefit all
caregivers and to mitigate the risks known to be associated with medical care. Items
such as checklists, toolkits, and specific education/simulation programs have been and
continue to be developed from this process.

3

Enclosure

Department of Veterans Affairs (VA) Comments to
Government Accountability Office (GAO) Draft Report
*"VA ADMINISTRATIVE INVESTIGATIONS: Improvements Needed in
Collecting and Sharing Information"*
(GAO-12-483)

Cornerstone Recognition Program. The Cornerstone Recognition Program began in fiscal year (FY) 2008 as an incentive to VHA facilities to complete stronger RCAs. The recognition criteria focus on timeliness and strength of actions, as well as reporting back on the impact of actions taken. Facilities may earn bronze, silver, or gold awards based on the number of RCAs completed and the quality of those RCAs. Seventy-one medical facilities achieved awards in FY 2008, 122 in FY 2009, and 129 in FY 2010. Since the program's inception, nearly 85 percent of all VA facilities have improved their patient safety efforts.

Healthcare Failure Mode Effect Analysis. Healthcare Failure Mode Effect Analysis (HFMEA) is based on a five-step process used by interdisciplinary teams to proactively evaluate a healthcare process. Specifically designed for use by healthcare professionals, the process offers users analytica tools such as flow diagramming, decision trees, and prioritized scoring systems. The tools enable users to proactively identify vulnerabilities that place patients at risk and deal with them before harm results.

Peer Review Program. The VHA Peer Review Program allows a peer or group of peers to critically review care performed by a clinician. The essential element of this process is to evaluate a selected episode of care and determine the necessity of specific actions recommended by the peer review process. Confidential communication is given to the provider regarding the results of the review as well as any recommended actions to improve performance. Occasionally, this process may identify systems and process issues that may require special consideration, investigation, and possibly administrative action on the part of the facility leadership. As a means of validating the internal peer review process with local clinical staff, VHA has retained the services of a national contractor with expertise in conducting peer review across all provider disciplines. Each quarter, samples of cases that have undergone internal peer review are audited from each VHA facility as part of the external secondary review process.

Patient Safety Training. VA's NCPS conducts an extensive patient safety training program including one to three day programs addressing topics such as developing and implementing an RCA team, hands-on training concerning the use of the VA NCPS confidential database, conducting a HFMEA, and using human factors engineering to improve the safety of the healthcare environment.

Medical Team Training. VA's NCPS developed the Medical Team Training (MTT) program to improve patient care outcomes through more effective communication and teamwork among providers. The need for these skills is noted from existing patient safety literature as well as lessons learned from VHA RCA cases. Since March 2005, the MTT program has facilitated more than 200 learning sessions involving more than 15,000 staff at VHA medical facilities nationwide.

4

Department of Veterans Affairs (VA) Comments to
Government Accountability Office (GAO) Draft Report
**"VA ADMINISTRATIVE INVESTIGATIONS: Improvements Needed in
Collecting and Sharing Information"**
(GAO-12-483)

Three studies published recently have verified skills learned through MTT result in
reduced annual surgical mortality rates and an overall decrease in the number and
severity of wrong site surgeries. For example, the October 20, 2010, study entitled
"Association Between Implementation of a Medical Team Training Program and
Surgical Mortality," published in the Journal of the American Medical Association,
conducted a retrospective study of VHA's MTT program. VHA's nationwide training
program required briefings and debriefings in the operating room and included
checklists as an integral part of this process. The study found an almost 50 percent
greater decrease in the annual surgical mortality rate in groups trained in MTT methods,
as opposed to untrained groups. The study also noted that the longer MTT had been
practiced at a medical facility, the greater the decrease in mortality.

Credentialing and Privileging. Standardized credentialing process for all licensed,
registered, and certified health care providers throughout the country ensures
consistency and quality. VA's credentialing and privileging system is a proactive
method to ensure high quality care.

The credentialing system:

- Is recognized throughout the industry for the software package's ability to share
  information and files, alert other VAMCs to "red flags" on providers who apply to
  multiple facilities, etc.;
- Provides reports and messages allowing for continuous monitoring of providers;
  and
- Enables VA networks throughout the country to have access to recognized
  experts in every medical specialty and profession.

Focused Professional Practice Evaluation and Ongoing Professional Practice
Evaluation. VHA has implemented the Focused Professional Practice Evaluation
process for new privileges and the Ongoing Professional Practice Evaluation process
for continued monitoring of provider competency that are measured against the six
general competencies of patient care, medical/clinical knowledge and procedures,
practice based learning and improvement, interpersonal and communication skills,
professionalism, and system based learning.

National Practitioner Data Bank. VHA has mandated participation in the National
Practitioner Data Bank's Continuous Query process for all privileged providers by all VA
facilities. This is considered a risk mitigation strategy since provider medical
malpractice payment and adverse action reports are delivered to the VA facility with an
active enrollment.

5

Enclosure

Department of Veterans Affairs (VA) Comments to
Government Accountability Office (GAO) Draft Report
*"VA ADMINISTRATIVE INVESTIGATIONS: Improvements Needed in
Collecting and Sharing Information"*
(GAO-12-483)

Accreditation and Facility Surveys. All VHA facilities are accredited by The Joint Commission. Joint Commission accreditation and certification is recognized nation-wide as a symbol of quality that reflects an organization's commitment to meeting certain performance standards. The accreditation and certification process includes scheduled and unscheduled reviews. VHA also participates in a variety of other accreditation programs. For example, VA Physical Medicine and Rehabilitation programs voluntarily submit to accreditation surveys by the Commission on Accreditation of Rehabilitation Facilities (CARF), an international independent, nonprofit accreditor of health and human services including medical rehabilitation. Approximately 80 VA rehabilitation programs are currently accredited for Comprehensive Integrated Inpatient Rehabilitation, Interdisciplinary Outpatient Care, Brain Injury Rehabilitation, Amputation Specialty Care, Interdisciplinary Pain Care, and Stroke Specialty Care. Accreditation through CARF also applies to Inpatient Blind Rehabilitation Centers and Outpatient Intermediate, Advanced, and Vision Impairment Services in Outpatient Rehabilitation programs.

Facility surveys are important tools that VHA uses to monitor the quality of care in VHA facilities. For example, the VHA Community Living Center (CLC) program conducts annual unannounced surveys to identify CLCs at risk including taking such action as educating staff toward improvement, consulting, and supporting the transformation of the culture of care. VHACO Office of Geriatrics and Extended Care carefully reviews the survey results to ensure appropriate follow up. If a certain level of findings is identified, the survey team does not leave the facility until the problem has been addressed.

Individual Tools. VHA uses individual tools in almost all disciplines to identify, address, and communicate about systemic concerns. Examples include:

- *Patient Safety Alerts and Advisories.* VA's NCPS publishes safety alerts or advisories on specific issues relating to equipment, medications, and procedures that might cause harm to our patients; these alerts and advisories are shared nationally and worldwide on VA's Intranet and Internet sites. Patient Safety Alerts communicate urgent notices that require immediate and specific action(s) by specific parties by a specified deadline. Advisories communicate recommendations and are more general in nature; implementation may be subject to local judgment.

- *Product Recall Office.* VHA's Product Recall Office manages recalls of all medical devices and products initiated by manufacturers or the Food and Drug Administration (FDA). Compliance, defined as removing recalled products from the supply chain, has risen to and is holding at 98 percent. The Product Recall

6

Department of Veterans Affairs (VA) Comments to
Government Accountability Office (GAO) Draft Report
*"VA ADMINISTRATIVE INVESTIGATIONS: Improvements Needed in
Collecting and Sharing Information"*
(GAO-12-483)

Office receives more than 12,500 recall notices from a variety of sources annually.

- *Quarterly Data Summary Reports.* These reports are used to monitor the status of each VA facility's reporting system. The data includes information on RCA reports, aggregate reviews, safety reports, outlier plots, actions, and event types by location. The quarterly summary report has been useful in identifying norms of event reporting and locations where event reporting cultures are struggling or thriving. Minimum expectations for reporting and development of a recognition program have been established in a large part by tracking these results over time.

- *Benchmarking Outcomes.* An example is the work of the Physical Medicine and Rehabilitation programs across VHA. These programs use the Functional Independence Measure tool, a valid and reliable industry standard, to measure rehabilitation outcomes. Data collected are submitted to the Uniform Data System for Medical Rehabilitation (UDSmr), a not-for-profit organization that maintains the world's largest database for medical rehabilitation outcomes. UDSmr provides quarterly reports to each facility that includes comparison to VA and private sector programs.

- *Office of Rural Health (ORH).* All ORH-funded projects are expected to follow established VHA program office quality of care protocols that apply to their projects. The Web-based ORH Management and Analysis Tool enables multiple individuals to access, report, view, and analyze project measures and milestones 24/7.

- *Office of Women's Health.* The Women's Assessment Tool for Comprehensive Health is completed at every site annually for validity of individual self-assessments.

- *Geriatrics and Extended Care.* Quality Indicators that are generated by Minimum Data Set requirements are reviewed locally each month and at VHACO quarterly.

- *Pharmacy.* VA has modernized the reporting of medication adverse events, which provide VA and FDA with early warning signals for potential side effects of medications. In addition to pharmacists' point of care review for each prescription, VA uses the VAMedSAFE program. Medication use evaluations for several categories of drugs are performed each year.

7

Department of Veterans Affairs (VA) Comments to
Government Accountability Office (GAO) Draft Report
*"VA ADMINISTRATIVE INVESTIGATIONS: Improvements Needed in
Collecting and Sharing Information"*
(GAO-12-483)

- *Mental Health Environment of Care Checklist.* This checklist was developed for VHA medical facilities to review inpatient mental health units for environmental hazards, decreasing the chance a patient could commit suicide or inflict self-harm. A 2010 article in the Joint Commission Journal on Quality and Patient

  Safety entitled "An Examination of the Effectiveness of a Mental Health Environment of Care Checklist," described the development of the Mental Health Environment of Care Checklist in VA hospitals during 2007 and 2008. The article reported, "113 VA facilities used the [. . .] Checklist to evaluate their mental health units, identifying and rating 7,642 hazards. At the end of the first year of the project, because of the checklist, 5,834 (76.3 percent) of these hazards had been abated by facilities; approximately 2 percent were identified as critical hazards, and another 27 percent were rated as serious."

The article also noted:

> "Unlike the general medical system in the United States, which is composed of thousands of independent hospitals developing idiosyncratic plans to manage risk the VA has the advantage of being an integrated system in which systemwide strategies can be deployed across all hospitals in the system. The use of a checklist is an explicit effort to reduce ambiguity of communication and implementation to mitigate patient risk and improve care."

8

Appendix III: GAO Contact and Staff Acknowledgments

GAO Contact	Debra A. Draper, (202) 512-7114 or draperd@gao.gov
Staff Acknowledgments	In addition to the contact named above, Janina Austin, Assistant Director; Jennie F. Apter; Julianne Flowers; Lisa Motley; Carmen Rivera-Lowitt; C. Jenna Sondhelm; and Brienne Tierney made key contributions to this report.

www.ingramcontent.com/pod-product-compliance
Lightning Source LLC
Chambersburg PA
CBHW080934290526

45795CB00007BA/2752